Breathing with the Mind

Kenneth Verity has worked and travelled extensively in the Far East. His interest in Haiku and Senryu began during the European tour of the work of Sengai, the Zen buddhist-priest, artist and poet, in the early 1960s. Later, after studying Zen with the Korean Master Seung Sahn and meeting the Shodo Master and teacher, Kampo Harada, he spent some time in Kyoto and Tokyo augmenting and completing *Breathing with the Mind*.

He is an initiate of the Mevlevi Order of Whirling Dervishes, who are based at Konya in Turkey. The combination of Sufi tradition, Zen practice and the mindstilling effect of meditation, have produced the author's unique insight, which is fully brought out in these brief and powerful poems.

He arranges Japanese visual and performing arts demonstrations in the Eastern Department (which he directs) at a large, International Arts Festival near Oxford, England, each year.

He tutors a thriving Writers' Group for professionals and runs stimulating and successful poetry workshops.

Breathing with the Mind

Verses in Senryu and Haiku Style

Kenneth Verity

E L E M E N T
Shaftesbury, Dorset ● Rockport, Massachusetts
Brisbane, Queensland

© Kenneth Verity 1993

Published in Great Britain in 1993 by
Element Books Limited
Longmead, Shaftesbury, Dorset

Published in the USA in 1993 by
Element, Inc
42 Broadway, Rockport, MA 01966

Published in Australia in 1993 by
Element Books Limited for
Jacaranda Wiley Limited
33 Park Road, Milton, Brisbane, 4064

Cover illustration by Ukiyo-e, Hosoda Eishi,
The courtesan Hanaôgi preparing to inscribe a fan, c. 1795,
Magna Books.
Cover design by Max Fairbrother
Typeset by Phil Payter Graphics, Southsea, Hants.
Printed in Great Britain by Redwood Books,
Trowbridge, Wiltshire

British Library Cataloguing in Publication
data available

Library of Congress Cataloging in Publication
data available

ISBN 1–85230–440–5

Contents

Illustration List

To Sumie Takahashi

Acknowledgements

I am grateful to the Trustees of the British Museum for their kind permission to reproduce some of the illustrations used in this book.

I acknowledge my indebtedness to the Kenkyusha, Japanese-English Dictionary (revised edition) which proved invaluable, particularly in the compilation of the glossary.

Introduction

The poetry in this book is easy to read, brief and to the point. It is based on a style called *haiku*, a name that comes from seventeenth century Japan. Haiku derives from *hokku*, meaning 'a hook'. The verses were so named because their brevity had led to the grouping, or linking, of several together in a chain or series. Each series had a header-poem or leading verse which stood on its own and became what we now call a haiku.

In form, the haiku consists of seventeen syllables or units, arranged in the pattern 5-7-5.

One of the most famous haiku in Japanese literature is a verse by the master, Matsuo Bashō (1644–94):

Furuike ya,   *An old pond*
Kawazu tobikomu,   *A frog jumps in –*
Mizu no oto.   *The sound of water!*

No translation quite catches the vitality and depth of the original. For the poet there was a special significance about the 'plop' as the frog entered the water.

The *senryu* was a popular form of verse writing that parodied the haiku but adhered to the same syllabic structure of 5-7-5. It reached maturity in Edo (now Tokyo) under Karai Senryu (1718–90) with whose name it became synonymous.

Haiku and senryu are identical in form but very different in content. Haiku are somewhat austere and tend to deal with the Natural World, for example, the seasons. In contrast, senryu are more relaxed and contain wry observations on everyday occurrences and the human condition.

The celebrated Eastern principle 'Less is more' is exemplified by senryu and haiku. With the brevity goes a subtle impact and a significance that yields its meaning to a few moments' reflection. For example:

> *A mouse darts forward to feed –*
> *And the silent owl*
> *Drops in to supper!*

Haiku and senryu have been known in Japan for hundreds of years and like proverbs have retained

their currency because they embody wisdom.
Most have precision, irony or wit.

> *Into her hair's raven blackness*
> *Have just appeared*
> *Some grey messengers …*

Haiku and senryu are simple to understand and
the poems in this book are immediately accessible
without introduction, other than to emphasize
that the statement must be complete within the
span of seventeen syllables. The verse usually
implies what has preceded the event described
and what might follow it. For example:

> *On his birthday*
> *The ferryman's boat*
> *Goes less straight across the river!*

None of the poems in the present volume is a
translation; each is an Anglo-Saxon original I
have written specially for this book. With some
notable exceptions, the Japanese originals rarely
survive translation without loss, and the unique
distinction of this poetic genre is best caught, in
English, by a fresh statement.

Each poem in this book is a complete experience, intended to stand alone. To emphasize this, they are not in sequence; nor are they grouped by subject. Haiku and senryu are not differentiated but the distinction is clearly brought out in the next section, 'History and Origins'.

What you read will, I hope, encourage you to write haiku of your own, but in the meantime, why not enjoy their style and perspective.

History and Origins

The brief succinct verse-form now known as *haiku* has a long history and can be traced back to the eleventh century. In turn, its antecedents go back further still and are to be found in an anthology of poetry called *The Manyōshū* or 'Collection of Ten Thousand Leaves'. This manuscript contains seventh and eighth century poems and is one of the richest storehouses of early Japanese literature. Its contents indicate the beginnings of syllabic development in Japanese verse. The English 'syllable' is not quite equivalent to the Japanese unit of sound duration but it is a convenient description.

Japanese poetry has always been distinctive and traditional. Before the sixteenth century, it flourished as an aristocratic art practised by gentlemen and ladies who adopted an almost ritualistic approach to an extended reciprocal exchange. Each writer attempted to eclipse the other by an excelling of wit or more skilful exploitation of classical allusion. But too often, a famous example or theme, taken as precedent in this formal exchange, was over-used to the point of sterility. The verse form employed was the *tanka* or *waka*. Both were identical in syllabic structure, that is, 5-7-5; 7-7 making a total of thirty-one syllables for each tanka or waka. Sometimes each verse was linked by subtle rules to any preceding or succeeding verses to form a chain-poem. The chain-poem so formed was called *renga* (renga means 'verse-linking'). Less serious renga, which later grew increasingly popular, were lighter in vein. These were called *haikai-renga*, or simply, *haikai*.

In 1603 the Tokugawa family established their shogunate (a shogun was a regent of the emperor, but the shogunate was, in effect, a hereditary military dictatorship) at Edo, the thriving ancestor of Tokyo, and Japan entered its third phase of feudalism. Throughout the Tokugawa Period (1603-1867) society and literature underwent gradual change. Poetry no longer remained the exclusive preserve of the establishment, and bourgeois society developed its own poetic form. This emerged from the chain-poem, haikai, the first verse of which was a three line seventeen-syllable verse called *hokku* ('a hook'). Eventually, the hokku became separate from the remainder of the poem and developed as an independent poetic genre known as *haiku*. The terms haikai, hokku and haiku are sometimes mistakenly used interchangeably for the seventeen-syllable haiku.

The haiku had always been popular with the ordinary people because its ideas and vocabulary were less constrained than the substance of the more formal aristocratic poetry. Originally, haikai were linked verses in which several poets had collaborated, composing 5-7-5 or 7-7 stanzas in alternation, generally extending the series to thirty-six or a hundred. The opening verse of 5-7-5 (the hokku) had often been written to stand alone, so that the haiku was not a radical departure in itself. The haiku began progressively to supersede the haikai in importance until the Meiji Period (1868-1912). During this period it was accepted as the acknowledged ordinary form of poetic expression.

One of the earlier and more important of the haiku poets was a former samurai, Bashō (1644-1694). He established himself as a professional haiku master at Edo, although always retaining a strong interest in haikai. His best known work is a poetic travel-diary of a trip to the northern provinces of Honshu, 'The Narrow Road to the North'.

Here is an example of this master's succinct but atmospheric work. He the writer provides the information; you the reader resonate with his images from within your imagination.

Asa-tsuyu ni yogorete suzushi uri no aoro

In the morning dew,
Covered in dirt, but quite fresh,
A muddy melon.

Bashō

Two other notable masters, Buson (1716-1783) and Issa (1763-1827), both of peasant origin, were more exclusively haiku poets.

Here is an example of each man's work:

Tagayasu ya tori sae nakanu yama kage-ni

Ploughing the field
In the shadow of a hill;
No bird is singing

Buson

Sumi no kumo anji na susu wa toranu zo yo

Spiders in corners,
Don't worry yourselves; I shall
Not be cleaning them
                              Issa

As the Japanese evolved their verse-form each new stage tended to begin with a strictly formal, almost religious severity, which later provoked a reaction. This in turn produced an identically structured verse-form but with a less restrictive content. This recurring developmental factor has always been a characteristic of Japanese poetry and it has determined the direction in which the evolving verse-forms moved. Just as the early seventeenth century haiku was a reaction against the waka, which had always omitted the unpoetic less palatable facts of life, so in the eighteenth century, there was a reaction against the haiku. The new form, called senryu, took the same syllabic measure (5-7-5) as the haiku, but its content was very different and the whole was less stylized. The distinction is quite fundamental. A haiku catches, in essence, a glimpse of the Natural Order; the senryu is a perceptive glance at human nature, a remarking of psychological insight. In both, we see something of significance through the agency of a detail. Both express what has been seen with a cool objectivity, but in the haiku, there is a non-involvement and remoteness; it avoids hyperbole, eroticism, passion, misdemeanour and idiosyncrasy. The senryu, on the other hand, includes all these and more, making no distinction between the sublime and the mundane. It brings in satire, wit, humour, exaggeration. But although there may be irony or sharpness, the best senryu carry a human warmth, a compassionate understanding, which only rarely degenerates into commiseration or sentimentality. That which is painful in life is not rejected or ignored; it is astringently, but not maliciously remarked; the observation is made and left at that. The proud may be deflated but there is no attack on the oppressed.

Both haiku and senryu imply a continuity of events before and after the moment of the poem, a characteristic inherited from their origins in haikai or linked-verse. Though brief in itself, the poem says much by focusing on a part of the whole which tells it all.

People generally think by means of concepts. A word represents a concept or thing and, although full of potential meaning, is rarely of use in isolation. Its meaning develops when the word or concept is related with others; the significance proceeds from the relationship. A harmonious arrangement produces a coherent expression, the very clarity of which may result in increased understanding. If the words, as sounds, are grouped in the context of metre, assonance, rhythm, rhyme, alliteration and so on, the statement could become poetry; when the substance of meaning is shaped in the form of poetry it gains penetration and might be memorable.

The haiku is all meaning. It has a directness, an immediacy, a potency which comes with the full impact of experience. It constitutes a true record of a vivid moment; sensation and experience are caught and held in poetry, yet haiku and senryu have few of the characteristics of that art-form. They do not rhyme. They have little rhythm; they are stark – yet they are undeniably poetry! The haiku is an understatement; its simplicity is deceptive for it says much in little. What it omits is as significant as what it includes.

It is not surprising that the same culture which gave rise to Zen also produced haiku. Certain characteristics of each are present in both, and a brief consideration of Zen Buddhism enlarges the understanding of haiku. The Zen sect emerged from a school of Mahayan Buddhism which flourished in China during the eighth century. Two centuries earlier, the Indian system had been brought to China where it encountered the indigenous thought and culture, particularly a religion of simple spontaneity and natural mysticism called Taoism. An integrating process occurred which resulted in a distinctive transformation of the Buddhist approach, giving rise to a Chinese religious form which reached its full development during the T'ang and Sung Periods. In the twelfth century it was introduced to Japan where, as the result of further modification, Zen became synonymous with a penetrative and practical understanding of Buddhism. It has become a way in which conceptual involvement is uncompromisingly thrust aside, and the essential is a first-hand knowing gained from immediate experience. The name Zen, an abbreviation of the Japanese word *zenna*, etymologically derives from the Chinese *chan-na* and in turn, from the sanskrit *dhyāna*. The word, in origin, meant: 'meditation, concentration, to centre the mind'; but the Zen practice constitutes very much more than this. It integrates the stillness of the inward turn of meditation and the activity of the outward turn to the physical world.

Buddhism promulgated three particular aspects of spiritual discipline which stemmed from an

Indian tradition with much earlier origins. These three aspects are:

Vinaya   discipline – the practical implementation of rules of conduct taught by Buddha to his followers.

Dhyāna   which Patanjali defined as concentration of the mind to avoid the scattering of mental energy.

Prajnā   Information, intelligence, discrimination, understanding, judgement, wisdom, knowledge.

Also, the related *jnāna*:
knowledge, true or superior knowledge, consciousness, organ of sense, the higher intelligence of man.

Prajnā is variously translated but is, in the context of Zen, considered to be the inner awakening of the intellect; the unrestricted connection of full consciousness directly with the senses. The Japanese use the word *satori*, and it is this awakening which is so strongly emphasized in Zen.

Satori is the inner shift of balance which shatters ignorance as awakening occurs, arousing knowledge of 'suchness' of reality now. In this reality and certainly not without it, there is detachment from ego-centred motivation. This alone liberates man from the inner qualitative residue of his actions. Zen is the art of being conscious of the truth by means of a living experience of it. The practice is to enter wholly into an action; the act is giving oneself. It is not a separate formal activity. As this entry becomes complete, practice and life wholly integrate; the merging becomes reality. The merging *is* the practice and the situation dissolves the ego. The implication of Zen is that unity in life is not achieved by revulsion against things or forms, but by a full entry into one's actions. The question is, how to achieve this entry. The significance of Zen is that separate methods practised in isolation from everyday living are simply a diversion. In Zen, the doer and the deed are undivided – dual aspects of a unity.

According to history the awakening in the activity has sometimes been achieved in drastic ways. A Zen master of the T'ang dynasty, Tokusan, used to say:

> *Whether you speak or do not speak,*
> *Thirty blows of my stick*
> *Just the same!*

There were to be no half-measures or there would be no rebirth. The man was jolted into the present, his mind emptied by the sudden impact on his awareness of immediacy. With the emptying of mind, ideas like individuality, I-me-mine, disappear. This can be a permanent new condition, hence the term re-birth. The brief moment of entry into activity, like the withdrawal into stillness in meditation, is the threshold of awakening to Reality, that is the permanence behind the transience.

In the silence is the numinous presence which fills all space; it is in everything. It is immanent. Connect with it, merge in it, be That! The essential is the oneness of the ego-less state, which does not exist as a duality – meditation and action. The ego-less response of no-mind, serene stillness in activity, inaction in action; these constitute 'being' not 'doing'. The immanent presence remains veiled by forms and substance; by movement and activity. It is the reality behind the changing transience of the world. There comes a moment when there is no difference between the reality in the 'individual' and the reality everywhere. There IS only one reality. When the immanent reality manifests it-self, which is yourself because there is no difference, then there is a re-birth indeed! Man no longer adds his personal overlay to the creation. He walks leaving no footsteps; performs deeds which leave no trace; and, being in the light of consciousness, casts no shadow.

To be absolutely clear about this, no diminution of human achievement is implied by this. The plays of Shakespeare and the discovery of general anaesthetics still stand at the forefront of benefit to the human race. But metaphors like 'writing on water' and 'walking leaving no footsteps' simply imply the abandonment of ego, not laying claim to results and not getting personally involved in what is done. In truth, we are merely the agents for what occurs. If we 'create' a garden do we also make the buds open and the grass grow?

Zen is concerned with the 'suchness' of things – that which is. What then, has the living experience to do with words? Obviously, a series of nouns hardly constitutes even the elements of sensory experience, but poetry is another matter. A poem is able to compel a flash of insight by conveying the integrated wholeness of an experience, whereas a noun merely offers the reader an opportunity to imagine something. A poem invites a sharing of knowledge and experience. In real poetry we look, not for decoration but for truth. A good writer, said Thomas Carlyle, makes us aware of things. Agreed, but surely not of forms only?

Poetry may direct the attention to the very substance which manifests as the forms; to the laws by which the forms arise; to the reality of the substance so formed; to the existence, itself, of that substance; and ultimately to the truth which that existence expresses.

The haiku has been a statement of reality for centuries in the language of Japan, but with modern haiku in the English language, the question of form arises. Is presentation to be in couplets or triplets; should rhyming be permitted? Since this Japanese form is based on seventeen syllables, should the English version conform unfailingly to 5-7-5 measure? Many of the haiku masters deviated from it. In practice, one finds that if 5-7-5 occurs naturally that is excellent; but if a haiku appears contrived, or if an inappropriate word is adopted simply for its syllabic measure, vitality is lost.

The haiku which constitute much of this book are neither so rigidly formal, nor so uncompromisingly stark, as the poems of the early masters. Such a formal purity would probably make them unacceptable to all but specialist readers. Suffice it to say that they, and the senryu, describe some aspect of reality expressed as a detail of creation or a glimpse of human behaviour, seen in the moment, and raising a veiled question or revealing a hidden significance. The haiku is not a new form but its place in Western literature is far from established. It is to be hoped that this situation will change, because this succinct poetry has a remarkable capacity for turning the mind in an unfamiliar direction, so stimulating thought and reflection.

Haiku and Senryu
Verses and Notes

> Breathing with the mind,
> Insight without concept comes
> By inspiration.
>   Shinri (1931-   )

Cock in a shower

Strutting round the farmyard,
The cockerel –
When did HE ever lay an egg?

Peering at the world
Through an idea; well pleased
 With what he sees!

❀

That child's mind
Is a blank sheet of paper!
 What are you writing on it?

❀

Birds gather
Nesting material; watching,
 I grow one year older.

As the calf was born,
The farmer's wife softly
Breathed a sigh of relief.

'I am God'
Thundered the teacher –
Although not quite in those words.

Although wanting a chicken –
The man, hungry today,
Must eat the egg.

This verse illustrates the tragedy of men who, although struggling to rise above mere subsistence level, are forced to eat next year's seed to feed this year's hunger.

She cuts growing flowers
To decorate the house –
Killing them gently.

The old shoemaker
Has acquired much of his wisdom –
From people's feet!

A specialist in anything reads significance into details which might escape most of us.

The potter sells space –
Shaped under his hand to forms
Of containing clay.

Like the calligrapher, who encloses beautifully proportioned space with his containing line, the maker of pots encloses a little of the universal space for people to put things into.

The grizzling child's
Icy fingers take a biscuit
From the mother's glove.

Blades of grass
Bent silently beneath the shoe,
Springing back – silently.

Meditating closed eyes,
Are you looking
At internal images?

One important form of meditation requires that the concentrated mind should be completely without images, concepts, words; that the interior screen should be totally clear. The verse is pointedly questioning the eyes of the meditator to ask if it really is meditation taking place in there, or simply dreaming and thinking.

Knowing he does not
Love her, she carefully
Avoids confirming it.

❀

Bronze smile, so frozen; a kiss
From your cold still lips, would taste
Of metal.

This verse is a response to the smile on the face of a beautiful woman, seemingly inviting a kiss but she is only a statue. Although the work is life-like and a piece of consummate Greek sculpture, sadly the exquisite lady is made of bronze.

❀

Although each grain of rice is tiny,
It is none the less rice
For that.

In any substance, each molecule is that very substance. This important fact often gets lost sight of when larger issues are under consideration.

Wanting to be loved,
She loves herself too much
To give any away.

❀

The incessant rain
Falling, whispering;
Each drop saying the same thing.

❀

This straw thatch,
Though it keeps out the rain,
Also obscures the eternal blue.

There are advantages and disadvantages in most things. This haiku is alerting us to look at the things we value most and see if they are not also impediments to our realization of ourselves.

Listening to her words;
Speculating on what she is
REALLY saying ...

When people communicate there are often other levels of meaning in a simple statement. How often does 'yes' imply a preferred 'no'? The addition of the word 'really' usually signals ambiguity.

❋

The miracle, water;
Two gases, yet they constitute
A liquid!

❋

The puddle dries slowly
And as it does so,
Is moistening the wind ...

This poem illustrates how something can be seen quite differently when observed from an unusual point of view.

The incense stick,
Slowly dissolving in fragrant smoke,
Merges with space …

Incense is a symbol of the dissolving and merging process in meditation where individuality dissolves into universality.

The water's freedom
Firmly locked up by frost;
This is more than stillness.

This verse alludes to the unfortunate hardness of heart which can occur in some religious people and some mystics. Stillness and detachment are one thing; rigidity and the state of being frozen quite another.

The shoe crushes the beetle;
Whose is the foot inside it
That doesn't notice?

We often blame inanimate objects for our own carelessness
and our mistakes.

'I follow,' said the blind man softly,
Using something more precious
Than eyes.

Seeing only this leaf,
With mind empty of ideas,
Knowing That!

A haiku about a very advanced level of meditative concen-
tration in which there is no thinking, no images, no words,
no conceptualization – just THAT.

Mist shrouds the woodland,
Hanging crystal beads on the webs;
These blackberries!

❀

The laurel is in flower!
Ears of wheat which no one will
Make into bread.

❀

That old fallen tree is being
Devoured by fungi;
But it takes time.

The natural world has its own slow but efficient way of clearing up debris and re-absorbing material to be freshly expressed in new forms.

'Listen,' he shouted;
But they were far too busy
Watching his ego.

❀

'Lip service' given
From the face – how genuine
Is body language?

❀

Nature, finishing
With things, re-uses the substance;
These whirling leaves!

In the natural world nothing is ever lost or destroyed. It is simply transformed into something else and re-expresses life in another form. Decaying leaves nourishing the living trees in woodland is an example of this.

He remembered her smile
After it had left her face –
Then he smiled.

✲

Beneath the torn edge
Of the fierce paper-tiger,
There is a man's foot!

✲

The wooden dragon
Gapes at the awestruck child;
Mind tries to devour it.

A child is seen trying to understand the significance of a carved fierce dragon.

The teacher shouted
Loudly at the sleeping pupil –
And woke himself.

❀

Discerning what she most
Wanted to hide from him,
He loved her for that!

❀

Foot-prints in the slushy snow –
That earlier passer-by;
Who was he?

The crisp rustling
Of her kimono,
    Gracious with femininity.

Sparrows pulling petals
From the cherry blossom –
What a pink snowfall!

Actress! Does anyone
Believe those illusions you
    Deceive yourself with?

Such lustrous, laughing eyes,
Revealing the clear radiance
    Of her soul.

The goldfish trace orange
Curves in water's liquidity ...
    This cool breeze!

Her love for him
Is his love for her – reflected
    Back into oneness.

Painters and lawyers
Can very swiftly alter
White into black!

❋

When you are thirsty
It is then too late to start
Digging the well.

❋

With 'wisdom' enough
To be one hundred years old –
Refugee children.

Refugee children, sadly, are often 'old' beyond their years.

It is difficult
To beat the dog after it
Starts to lick your hand.

❀

Restlessly busy,
The old go-between wears out
A thousand sandals.

❀

Some pots have lids that
Do not fit; but some pots just
Never fit the lids!

Living together, conforming, being individual, acknowledging uniqueness; these things seem to depend on interpretation and the point of view.

The Lovers Chu-bei and Umegawa

In love, each using
The smallness of the umbrella
To get closer.

All the others are
Only the others, whereas,
    I, of course, am me!

❀

At first he drinks wine,
Then wine begins to drink wine;
    At last, wine drinks him!

❀

She's chasing the cat;
It would have been easier
    To cover the fish!

As the pheasant 'honks',
The safety catch is being
Silently released!

❀

The nail that raises
Its head, is the very one
Which gets hammered down.

These two statements are related. The pheasant betrays its
presence in concealment; the nail stands out inviting notice.
Yet if it were not for the mistakes of evil doers and the
preparedness of people like Alexander Solzhenitsyn to stand
out against the hammer, the world would be a poorer place.

All the washing is out and blowing well!
Then the line snaps –
She breaks too!

❀

Purposefully, this
Tiny ant goes somewhere – but
Where did it come from?

❀

Sometimes buying it
Turns out to be cheaper than
Accepting a gift.

There are many levels of valuation and there have been some tragic examples of compromised integrity, for trivial so-called gifts. Also, obligation to bearers of gifts have a nasty habit of extending interminably. A baited hook is usually attached to a line!

Two red shoes, silently
Descending the staircase;
Quite delicious!

Ready to love –
But such a man is
Just an idea in her mind.

Gnarled old fingers claw up
Swatches of scratchy wheat-straw;
This too costly bread!

Adjusting her comb,
Peering into the mirror
At her transience …

Certain he was in the right,
The teacher had
Made his second mistake.

Caught in the act –
Confusing even himself
With all the explaining!

Every parent knows the efforts of young children to talk themselves out of trouble when caught in a misdemeanour.

Nobody just sits
There, while the adjoining
Dwelling is burning down!

The old forget, the
Young do not yet know; so who
Perceives the present?

The calligrapher,
Producing consummate work,
Knows well his best brush.

The novice rider,
Softly whispering her prayers
Into her pony's ear …

❄

She loves her husband –
And her children;
But of course, it isn't the same!

❄

The child's jerky brush
Paints plum-blossom, but mind
Creates a child painting.

Two levels of perception are implied here. The child learning to represent things and the observer projecting at a more sophisticated level.

These similar pots –
Different; uniqueness
Will not be mass-produced!

The pots made by the peasant are simple but each one is individual and different.

Even the growing plants,
Languid in this summer air
Droop with torpor.

A falling leaf can go
In any direction –
Chosen by the wind.

What we call 'freedom' is usually the compulsion of outside forces or our own inner conditioning.

Hurrying to meet him,
Her heart runs ahead;
No rest there to calm it!

With his arrival,
She senses the hostile clock prepare
To run faster.

Lovers have always been aware of the slow passage of time prior to their meeting and its fleeting elapse while they are together.

She is delight!
Moving with the total loveliness
Of woman.

❈

A twig snaps underfoot
With a mind-emptying 'crack'!
And I am That.

Ordinarily, the sound of a twig breaking beneath the foot
would not have much impact. But there are those moments
when we are in natural surroundings and are so openly
receptive that the mind is suddenly emptied totally of mun-
dane thoughts and concerns. When we are that open, a tiny
sound like the one in the haiku is all that is necessary to
centre attention instantly, at full power.

Fullness of grace, and a
Longing to serve him, especially –
Her love.

❁

Back, bent over the
Mud of the paddy fields –
Is this the cost of rice?

❁

The spider spins, no thought
Of flies; the fly lives,
Oblivious of webs.

In the natural world things just happen but human beings
like to insert 'because' into the sequence of interactions.
Cause and effect are two sides of the same event.

Tenderly the mother
Cradles her child, birth pangs
Transmuted to love!

Sheep chew and stare;
But then, to chew and stare
Is interesting to sheep.

Along the street
Paper-lanterns swinging gently;
Is it mind that moves?

This is a celebrated Zen conundrum. If you perceive a banner moving in the wind, is the banner moving or the wind – or your mind?

The axe-blade sinks
Deeply into the splitting log,
Releasing fragrance.

❀

The student fell
Fast asleep at his daily practice
Of waking up.

Unless the freshness and spontaneity of process is kept alive in the moment now, it can eventually turn full cycle and our effort achieves the opposite of our intention.

❀

The priest's lacquered clogs,
Imbued with his dignity,
Clop, clop, discreetly.

A Shinto priest, walking high on thick wooden clogs, is noticed on his way to an important ceremony at the main temple of Kurama.

Empty shoes wait
Outside the shrine; minds
Full, unfortunately, inside.

Tree, too old and stiff to bend,
Throwing your branches away
In the storm!

Those umbrellas
Moving in gentle rain,
Have their own liquidity!

The poet sees a delicious interaction in the undulating lines of Japanese umbrellas, moving and rippling through the liquid, falling rain.

A courtesan and her reflection

Laying down her mirror,
She looks sadly from the present
To the past.

Having to ask him if
He loved her, she knew in her heart
He didn't.

The action is deferred – for now,
Waiting the
Right opportunity!

Singing softly as she works,
Polishing HIM
In the gleaming surface!

The almond tree's snowflakes
Have settled;
Why is the sun not melting them?

Bringing this hammer down
Attentively, I become –
A hammer-blow!

Conceptual thinking separates us from people and things. Although we may desire to be in total harmony with an object or another person, we seem to have to make a 'bridge' or establish a relationship. This is because we are thinking of ourselves as separate beings instead of realizing that we all exist in unity! This poem indicates a state of no separation, no difference; a merging where the hammer-blow and the striker are one.

Snow is here today
And gone tomorrow; but then
Such things never last.

❀

Dolls Festival –
Indulgent parents hard at play
With their human toys!

The Dolls Festival (Hina-Matsuri) takes place on the third day of the third month. (The ancient Chinese attached great significance to the coincidence of number of days and month.) On this day, tiers of attractive dolls are displayed on shelves in a small shrine or a simple stand. Offerings of peach blossom, with sweet sake and white sake, are placed before the dolls and the young girls in their kimonos pay their respects. Friends are invited to drink white sake as a prayer for good health in the ensuing year.

She has no more to win him
Than she has to make
The sun rise at dawn!

❋

The young boy gazes
At the billowing carp;
Symbol, urging him on.

This senryu refers to the Boys' Festival (Kio-nobori: carp banners). The fifth day of the fifth month is an important festival, Tango no Sekku (The Fifth of the Fifth). The word tango at one time signified the first occurrence of a 'double-fifth'. Particularly in towns, carp-banners are to be seen at about the time of Tango no Sekku, floating on the breeze high in the May sky. These cloth or paper streamers shaped like carp, belly out like wind-socks and seem to swim undulatingly against the current of a stream. The eldest son has a large one, and they progressively diminish in size to a tiny one for the baby. There is a legend that the carp, like the salmon, has to fight upstream to breed and the banners symbolize, and are intended to promote, a corresponding manliness in overcoming life's difficulties.

Still laden with unwanted berries –
The trees, after
This mild winter.

Those glistening teeth of hers!
Moistened with that liquidity,
Her laughter.

Gentle summer rain,
Indifferently moistening
All it touches …

Like the sun, rain gives its nourishing wetness to everything
without discrimination or criticism.

So charged to overflowing
With love, her full heart
    Constrains her breathing.

❋

    Wind exerts its pressure
On all things; most yield, but some fall –
    How it blows!

The woodcutter's sweat
Soaking the faggots –
His fire consumed by fuel!

❀

New Year's Day!
This old tree does not
Seem to notice any difference.

The solar calendar places the 'beginning' of the year in what is, really, mid-winter. In 1872, during the fifth year of the Meiji Period, Japan adopted the solar calendar. Prior to this, the passage of days and years was observed against the lunar calendar which came from China. This gave rise, in some areas, to the celebration of New Year three times as annual rituals adapted to the new calendar. The Greater New Year is an observance based on the traditional Chinese calendar, and New Year greetings are exchanged during this period.

Many rites observed during the Lesser New Year are associated with agriculture, and are concentrated in the days either side of the fifteenth of the first month. Also, in the first month, there is a ceremony foreshadowing the rice-planting and an old observance in which replicas of agricultural implements are offered to the gods.

Seba

Sometimes the current
Is with you, and sometimes against;
Who keeps changing it?

Striving to create
The impression she wants –
She gives another one.

❀

'Love me forever' she pleaded –
Seeking some
Temporary comfort.

❀

Self-conscious young person,
Never mind us – someone else
Is watching you!

Children simultaneously 'play to the gallery' and suffer embarrassment from being observed. There is another observer – the Witness or universal presence, which is always in the present.

To her lover she
Complains about having to
Lie to her husband!

❀

'There is only you'
She murmurs; 'I didn't really
Love all the others!'

❀

The earthquake shakes
Down the hovel with the palace –
Indifferently.

Bamboo

Bending with the wind
The bamboo bowed, gracefully,
But it is straight now!

> *This worm drying out on the pavement,*
> *Tempted too far*
> *By the moisture!*

The worm, stranded and dehydrating, is a familiar sight after a warm showery night. Like a brief echo of Wolsey's great speech of farewell in Act III of Shakespeare's *Henry VIII*, this haiku reminds us of the hazard of moving out of place simply because conditions are temporarily favourable.

> *Two frogs are mating*
> *On the bottom of this pond;*
> *Do they enjoy it?*

> *Why the impatience?*
> *The first occasion may be*
> *Enjoyed only once.*

Waiting can be tantalizing, delicious, nourishing, instructive and sometimes, frustrating. Nevertheless, there IS only one first time.

The Zen master deftly
Struck the student with his stick –
To rouse insight!

Time lurks like a thief
Just outside the moment 'now' –
Waiting to steal life.

The full moon in this puddle –
Leaving little room
For anything else!

There are many meanings in this haiku. Some ideas fill the mind, overshadowing whatever else is there. What if, like the moon in the puddle, they are ideas based on illusion?

The poetess Ono no Komachi in court dress

The edge of her gown
Still, momentarily,
Brushing the closing door.

> *The protesting cart-wheel*
> *Asks urgently for some grease –*
> *In a loud voice!*

It is said that vibration constitutes substance and shapes it into forms. Some vibrations are audible as sound and all sound is a language to those who can interpret its significance. In this senryu, the wheel 'speaks' as though in pain.

> *As her outer beauty declines,*
> *Her inner radiance*
> *Increases.*

> *Water, flowing only*
> *Downwards, ultimately*
> *Always comes to rest.*

There is a natural direction for everything.

The old stone lantern
Touched by the pine branch –
    They don't shiver in this wind!

Deeply in love with her,
He gazes in her direction
    Now and then.

The snow drifts,
Gathering the crystal beauty of
    Water into heaps!

Looking into her eyes,
I see at once that the soul
Does have windows!

❀

The thrush tugs fiercely
On the worm – which suddenly
Becomes a meal!

❀

The setting sun;
Rooks, still in the elm;
The mind enters meditation …

At sunset there is a changeover point in Nature's activity which seems a natural time to begin meditation . . .

She is him, he her;
What then is this 'difference',
Male and female?

❃

Child, gazing at nothing
In particular; have you
Conquered desire?

Everyone desires to experience pleasure and, if possible, to reduce or avoid pain. Because desires are said to be the cause of both and are seen as distractions, the Buddhist tries to conquer desire. The poem is alluding to this.

The strong winds have
Broken the chrysanthemums –
But they don't seem to mind.

❋

Tea ceremony –
Ritual form, releasing
Spontaneity.

The Tea Ceremony, called *Chanoyu* in Japanese, is the art of preparing and serving a bitter tea of lightly ground leaves called *matcha*, served in a cup called *chawan*. *Chado*, or the Way of Tea, has an unbroken tradition of four hundred years and, potentially, is a rigorous spiritual discipline for training the body and mind in awareness.

The great master, Sen-no-Rikyu, summarized the principles of the discipline of Tea into four concepts: *Wa* (harmony) a feeling of oneness with nature and people; *Kei* (respect) naturally arising from gratitude; *Sei* (purity) cleanliness and orderliness in both the physical and spiritual sense; *Jaku* (tranquility).

The underlying philosophy of the Way of Tea is a rich and unique synthesis of Oriental cultural and religious tradition. It is intended to increase spiritual awareness and inner peace.

Fish, vacantly gulping –
Like a child's mind, taking
Everything that comes.

As we grow older we gain discernment but, inevitably, we sometimes filter out beneficial influences by our editing of stimuli.

The bamboo, stirring in the wind
Whispers something;
YOU know what it says!

Instant to instant,
Whatever attracts the mind
Is THAT in disguise.

If the reality which lies behind appearances is to be alluded to without conceptualizing, it is often referred to simply as 'That'.

Discreetly lowering her eyes,
She has raised in him
  Expectation.

Swiftly cleaning the house;
One eye on the dirt,
  The other on the clock.

A fly blunders
Into the web, which implies
  That a spider is waiting!

The bright eyed squirrel,
Like a miser,
   Buries yet another acorn.

❀

Claiming our life as our own,
Introduces into it
   Fear of loss.

❀

Needing love,
But closing the source
   With her imperious demanding.

The young rider spurs on the horse,
Urging it to show
   Her at her best.

'Life must go on' she said,
Her piercing words
   Deadly with finality.

Dearth in the relationship,
Her ungiving is now
   Taking too much.

Ducks in Flowing Water, detail

A roosting mallard
Seized by the fox
Quacks out its life despairingly …

The sculptor cuts away
All that conceals the shape
He is releasing!

Like a brash freebooter
Seeking treasure;
He the thief, she the plunder!

The Persian carpet –
Its beauty marred by
The drudgery of weaving.

A kind of blindness,
Exchanging his integrity
For two bright eyes!

'I want to give you everything,'
He said to her,
Taking her freedom.

Trust growing,
Her insurances against
Imagined hurt not needed.

In love's combat,
Overcoming his strength
By her complete surrender.

In her mirror, now,
She sees the past's farewell
And the future's greeting.

The old craftsman,
His life ebbing into
Objects which will outlive him!

Desperately needing support,
Mistaking silent strength
 For weakness.

Love, which could have renewed them both
But, laden with conditions,
 Dying …

My horse at full gallop
Little knows how I esteem
 Sure footedness!

What the artist sees, he paints:
But the unseen
  Eludes more than his brush!

He learned to give so generously,
By receiving so much
  From her.

'Calm down' he said
Now that HIS turbulence
  Was attracting attention.

See blue sky
Without the concepts, 'blue' and 'sky',
　　Perceive reality.

❀

'I want to share my life
With you,' he said,
　　Offering her selfishness.

❀

Wanting something for herself
But willing to give first,
　　Gaining her wish.

When the mind is still,
Like a mirror, it reflects
What is really there!

❋

His seige of her having failed,
He won her –
By surrendering himself!

Martial metaphors which portray the male as aggressively forcing capitulation from the female, ignore the fact that in a loving relationship the male surrenders too. Both surrender their individual egos to a unity which dissolves their separation.

A pervading stillness,
With mind moving not at all;
This deep silence!

❋

On his way to her,
Longing for the future to become –
The present!

❋

Meditating and
Resplendent in the sunlight –
This water-lily.

Mind-conditioning meditation was imported to Japan from India via China. After a period of concentration and the transcendence of conceptualizing, the 'individual' may merge into the Universal. The water-lily, not able to think of itself as separate in the Oneness of Nature, is already merged in that universality. In a sense, it is permanently 'meditating' and this is the point of the haiku.

Cormorant on a Stump

No post, however proud,
Can cast a shadow of itself
At midday.

Samādhi (a Sanskrit word) is the merging of individuality into the Universal. The sense of individual existence (ahankāra in Sanskrit) dissolves at this level of transcendence, and the ego (like the post in the haiku) casts no shadow.

Busily stooking corn sheaves,
The peasant is counting
  His sacks of flour.

Displaying good taste,
Filling his bag with just the best –
  The housebreaker.

In the space of a marriage-bed,
They drifted apart
  A thousand miles!

The tears stream down,
Drowning even the roots of
Her unrequited love.

Biting into the bark
With a ringing moist thud,
The young woodman's axe.

The master,
Hearing very well the student's question,
Says nothing – loudly!

Effective communication is often a meaningful silence – especially in Zen Buddhism.

No master can rule,
Without occasionally
Playing deaf and blind.

People with the same
Illness are not short of
Something to talk about.

The Buddhist novice
Took a razor to his head –
But now shaves his mind.

The young Buddhist novice by shaving his head signals to the world, and to himself, that his mind is now to be divested of everyday worldly matters.

The dyer's hands show
Traces of the colour he was
Working with today.

One meaning of this statement is that the body often
indicates how we have lived our lives and the events that
have happened to us. It is not a criticism, but the hands of a
market-gardener and those of a bank clerk will disclose very
different activities.

From indigo comes
Blue dye, its hue more blue than
Indigo itself.

Dilution is not necessarily weakness or diminution. Some-
times the 'working strength' of a substance is its utility
and beauty for mankind. The beauty of the blue colour
elicited from indigo by dilution, is illustrative of an impor-
tant principle.

Japanese calligraphy in Gyōshū script.
This beautiful piece of calligraphy, produced for the author
by the Master, Kampo Harada, means 'love'.

Ink, significantly black
On paper's whiteness –
This creative act!

The black mark on white paper is one of the most symbolic creative acts possible. The calligrapher puts something where there was nothing; the virgin paper is 'seeded' by a vigorous, positive stroke; the spaces contained by the embracing lines are as important as the letters themselves.

The carp swims slowly
Because going nowhere
    Always takes a long time.

The bully – note his
Excessive deference to
    Those whom HE respects.

By the busy road
A laden almond tree – the
    Nuts will be bitter!

Bring down a great tree,
And with it will be lost its
Canopy of shade!

It is a long journey
From the mulberry leaf
To the silken gown.

Sharpening the edge,
But wearing away the blade –
The old knife-grinder.

Using things and maintaining their function is to consume them – life is like that . . .

The centipede does
Not give up walking because
It has one bad leg!

❀

Is not each dead child
Considered beautiful by
Its grieving parents?

❀

There is little point
In mending the West wall with
Stones from the East wall!

Anger! A moment's
Control now could obviate
A year of anguish ...

❀

If the doctors say
You will die young, prepare
Yourself for a long life.

❀

At the base of the
Large tree, rarely feeling frost –
The sheltering grass.

Benign protective largeness often safeguards the lesser or smaller creatures. This is a reminder of the duty the strong have towards the weak.

Ox tilling the field –
It is the fleet-footed horse
That will eat the grain!

When a sparrow finds
Its way into the grain-store
It soon stops chirping!

Just a few grains of
Sugar will bring a nestful
Of ants to the sack.

Never look into
A well with your enemy
Standing at your side!

✽

The dawn will not fail
To appear because one cock
Chances not to crow!

✽

The eminent man
Is unconcerned by the flaws
In less able men.

The feckless dreamer
Thinks he can turn somersaults
In a walnut shell!

What is harvested
At sea, inevitably
Must be sold on land.

To be servant to
An emperor, is like sleeping
With a tiger.

Many a Tudor noble in the entourage of Henry VIII would empathize with the metaphor of this Japanese courtier.

Who can know at dawn
What will have befallen them
By nightfall!

Only by consuming
Itself, does the candle
Give light to others.

Extreme deference
Is a sure indication
Of a large ego!

Those who believe that they have a personal self which will
benefit from preferment have very supple knees . . .

Now ready to thank
Their parents – the couple with
A child of their own!

❀

Confess ignorance,
It shows once; veiled, it
Will show many times.

❀

The pheasant, good at
Hiding its head, usually
Forgets its tail!

Seller of Fortune-telling Poems

After the string is
Released, the speeding arrow
Cannot be brought back.

The rich are often
Diligent; the very rich
Are superstitious!

❀

Needing an extra
Day, she got up at dawn three
Times in succession!

❀

Glimpsing his neighbour
In the fruit garden – nobly
He looks the other way!

People with a sense of proportion intervene only when it is necessary. The price of good relations sometimes means turning a blind eye; it might also involve a small loss occasionally . . .

A fear of women
Often causes the bully
To belittle them.

Talking it over
Beforehand, avoiding the
Risk of rejection …

If the man himself
Is upright, pay no heed
To his bent shadow!

There are many meanings in this statement. It is a reminder that undue weight need not be given to the age of the person. The behaviour lapse does not mean, necessarily, that the person is all bad. The ego is inevitably a distortion.

Lady with Fan

Inwardly calm,
Seeing HIM, her fingers
Twirl her hair distractedly.

> In order to gain
> Its drink of milk, the lamb must
> First kneel on the ground.

The mature lamb, still trying to get an easy meal, has to accommodate its bulk and self importance . . .

❋

> Fire in nine places;
> Sooner or later, smoke will
> Be seen at a tenth!

What people want to see and cannot find, they are likely to imagine.

Composing Senryu and Haiku

This final section offers thoughts and suggestions on how to set about composing these short poems. For simplicity, and to avoid repetition, the term haiku will be used to signify both haiku and senryu unless specifically distinguished.

This does not seem a good moment to be beset by rules and constraints. You will, however, want to begin with a good standard of composition. There are a few simple characteristics of haiku and senryu which ought to be borne in mind and, even at the beginning, should constitute basic requirements. These have been condensed into a few guiding principles:

There should be seventeen syllables in each poem. These are usually arranged to give the following pattern:

Five
Seven
Five

The event described should be something currently taking place, not something in the past.

Haiku report a natural event like the seasons; senryu can contain reference to almost anything else!

These poems particularize a happening; they are not usually a generalization.

Keep the idea simple; let the contrast of dream and reality be sharp. Tell the reader what *you* saw, felt, knew in the present moment.

You may be surprised by how well the poem expresses the emotional flavour roused in you by the event or detail seen. It may also reveal how integrated you, as an individual, were with the Natural World in that moment of heightened awareness.

MAKING A START

The haiku is such a pithy essential statement that merely writing a few relevant words about something constitutes the basis of a haiku. Of course it is the 'something' that gives the significance and this will be considered later.

The haiku is an austere, formal statement and in its strictly pure form, subject matter is, by convention, limited to Nature or religious matters. It often begins with an observation or musing; then concludes sharply with a contrasting realization. For example, someone is watching swallows preparing for migration; then a sharp gust of cold wind strikes the back of the neck and rouses the observer from reverie.

> *Swallows twitter excitedly*
> *On the telephone wires –*
> *This east wind!*

The observation, its significance and its emotional flavour must all be contained within seventeen syllables. However, in this haiku I have deliberately waived the 5-7-5 structure to obtain the scene setting statement:

> *Swallows twitter excitedly …*

which conveys the sound they make, their fluttering restlessness and a typical gathering place.

The last line,

> *This east wind!*

makes the poem a haiku, carries the impact of summer's departure and implies the onset of autumn. It seems to me that to add two more syllables to this would weaken its terseness.

To reassure you that I respect the rules, here is a poem with 5-7-5 structure:

Bringing an autumn
To these delicate petals,
This boisterous March wind!

In senryu the subject matter may be widened almost totally and, typically, might offer a wry comment on human behaviour, highlight the irony of human foibles, or introduce an emotional colour, for example, pathos.

When writing in English it seems preferable to count the syllables as *spoken* rather than as *written*, for example, 'secretary' is written with four syllables but many people pronounce it with three. Or, similarly, the word 'sententious' has a suffix which is contracted in speech.

However, leave aside such niceties if you wish. Just describe something, explain something, communicate something. Write a few words, make your point; touch on the irony, humour or the unusualness of what you've seen, and you have begun your first haiku. Distil your statement, shape it into three lines, reduce to seventeen syllables and you have finished your first haiku.

STRUCTURING THE HAIKU

Classical haiku were governed by strict rules but if these precise, Japanese-style statements are being written for enjoyment then too strict an adherence to the classical style is not essential. However, ideally the seventeen-syllable rule should not be broken.

It is the discipline of keeping within this constraint that sharpens the mental focus and generates the felicities of utterance and brilliance of some early examples of the genre. One is reminded of Shaw's apology for writing a long letter because he did not have time to write a short one. Distilling and refining the verse presents a challenge to the writer and gives enjoyment, as well as a shared experience, to the reader. So it is stimulating as well as a useful control to maintain the precise measure of seventeen syllables.

Set out the haiku in three lines, and aim for 5-7-5 if you want deliberately to limit your freedom and make the work more challenging!

When laying out the verse for shaping and reduction it is useful to delineate each phrase or clause and indicate to yourself the number of syllables thus:

| *at once* | *instantaneously* | *in an instant* |
| 2 | 6 | 4 |

This will spare you the tedium of having to keep counting as you reduce or extend, or when ascertaining where you can gain or lose a syllable.

Synonyms are one way of reducing syllables but words are not usually simply interchangeable. Subtleties of meaning are often finely graded and the use of an imprecise alternative will blur the sharpness of the haiku.

With practice you will be able to make a simple, potent utterance of seventeen syllables with no difficulty. Then without loosening structural succinctness you may sharpen the focus or shift the emphasis to achieve the desired impact. Even though brevity means a loss of lyricism, the formal lucidity of the haiku has a certain elegance.

CHOOSING THE SUBJECT

In the nature of things, the subjects of haiku and senryu tend to choose themselves since they are a distillation of life experience. Every perceptive person has glimpses of vital significance, flashes of insight, moments of penetration. All of us can recall memorable events or important minor occurrences which have left an indelible mark in memory.

These are neither rare nor infrequent but unless we are tuned to their possibility the moment may be missed and, like Shakespeare's lightning flash, be gone ere it has lightened.

These happenings are often of startling brevity, but it is this tantalizingly elusive quality which makes us so grateful for even the glimpse. Some care is needed here, for few of us can linger on something so ephemeral without spoiling it with a personal claim or an attempt at analysis that mars even as it examines. Fortunately, describing something need not destroy it. Unlike analysis, dissection or explanation, a concise account in words may catch and permanently hold the essence leaving the elusive 'something' intact.

With the formality of the haiku or the wide latitude of the senryu at our disposal, any subject may be the point of your poem. If something was significant for you, say so. Celebrate your moment of understanding or insight with a haiku!

Once you make a start, ideas for subjects will tend to arise out of memory and you will recall a vital moment of insight or remember an observed significance. Sit quietly with pad and pencil to hand, close the eyes and let such moments come. A trigger word will suffice to mark them for use; reflection and recall may continue uninterrupted.

CATCHING THE ESSENCE

A flabby prose description engages the reader only loosely with the subject described. In contrast, tautness may arrest attention, deepen involvement and secure the interest. The haiku leaves little room for prolixity but emphasis can be shifted considerably, even in so short a space. To illustrate this, two different examples of the same incident follow.

The pike lurks impassively;
With deft swiftness
It terminates a life!

The pike lies in wait;
Expressionless, its jaws
Snap over a minnow.

You may feel greater identity with the victim in the second haiku simply because identification has been more sharply focused.

A small but vital change can increase sympathy, heighten meaning, or convey more colour. With words we can intensify the awareness of the reader, engage feeling, stimulate the sensory response, rouse the capacity to resonate with subtler vibrations; all by selecting the precise word for our purpose. Attempting to capture the ephemeral in words, or distilling the essence of an observed moment, is an exacting but rewarding process. As well as honing the cutting edge of verbal expression it increases sensitivity to the myriad stimuli that play on the senses. This in turn may arouse a subtler response to phenomena and lead to more penetrating insight into the veiled significance of events.

DISTILLING THE MEANING

If an incident offers a glimpse of powerful insight or a moment has been held in the memory by the needle-sharp focus with which something was seen, the words to describe it can almost always be found. Nuances of significance or fine shades of meaning can be conveyed by selecting, with precision, the exact word you want. Only *you* know what you saw, or what you understood, in that extraordinary moment – the entire language waits to serve your creative discernment.

As the words you use powerfully converge on the meaning or import of what you want to say, you will know with a growing certainty that you have concentrated verbal description sufficiently to convey cogently your experience or insight.

If only one word will do but its use will exceed the syllable constraint, reconstruct the verse or change something else – perhaps a syllable can be gained by a more accurate choice of word elsewhere in your statement.

STIMULATING CREATIVITY

Creativity cannot be commanded but it can be invited by a receptive openness, attending with the mind still and clear. Inspiration (a creative breathing in) is powerful but unforced. It is not summoned but, rather, courted. Enthusiasm often produces a good 'environment' for creativity to manifest. Why not allow optimism, founded on your uniqueness and freshness to haiku writing, to enhance your creative potential!

Sitting in a place of natural beauty will often set up a resonance which tunes the mind and may well permit you to make a connection, through the emotional memory, with creativity. If insight does occur it is strangely immediate, so that the awakened memory of an earlier moment of perception is very much in the here and now. The Zen-like immediacy has that combined quality of now and eternity which the haiku so often highlights with its direct pointing to reality.

Sometimes music will stimulate a current of creativity. Its themes, resonances and melodies may charm open the creative dimension in our being. But beware of dreaming;

just listen openly, without the vague drifting that so often accompanies listening to music. If you want to drift – that's fine; it's just unlikely to produce any haiku!

Proximity to flowers, flowing water, panoramic distant views, all have their effect and may engage that vital stimulus to the creative flow.

STYLE

You need not waste energy wondering if your haiku will have stylistic impact. Every individual is unique, for all that there may be similarities, and your haiku style will reflect your uniqueness. *Your* experience conveyed in *your* approach will distil into a style solely your own.

Your imagery may carry an uncommon emphasis. For instance, one person may use a great number of gustatory similes and metaphors, frequently alluding to the taste of things, such as likening events to a feast or a banquet. For another, whose emphasis is auditory, the air is full of sounds.

Your own style awaits discovery and this is exciting and stimulating. Remember, your vision is singularly yours and your style an expression of your individuality.

The concealing art is the ability first to focus finely on what has been perceived and then to convey that conception in just a few words. Just let the words come and allow their cutting edge to carry the incisiveness of your original vision.

Finally, if you are wondering what your first haiku should be about, I wonder if you have ever seen a heavily-laden woman just miss the bus; or noticed how there is always one last leaf on the tree; or observed the trusting way a child holds its father's hand . . .

This is probably more than enough to enable you to make a fully effective entry into the process of creating haiku and senryu. I will conclude with some words of D.T. Suzuki:

> *'It is the poet who transforms the*
> *everyday life of prosaic-minded*
> *people into something unique,*
> *because it is the poet who sees*
> *the beautiful in the ordinary.'*

Glossary and
Supplementary Notes

This section augments and develops meanings given elsewhere in this volume and adds several further definitions. The terms listed give an insight into the background to Japanese poetry, its aesthetic ambience and the Zen Buddhist concepts which have tended to influence development of the *haiku*.

Aware: 'the suffering in things – the pathos of nature'; also 'the capacity to be touched with pity'. There is the implication of a sensitivity to the appreciation of this quality in natural things. For example, broken chrysanthemums after an autumn storm might have this sad beauty.

Chōka: 'long poem' structured in alternative 5 and 7 syllables, the whole concluding with an extra 7 syllable line. Often succeeded by one or more *envoy* poems in *tanka* form. The *chōka* flourished in the eighth century and some fine examples occur in *The Manyōshū*.

Envoy: see *Hanka*.

Hakanai: 'passing, fleeting, transient' and the derived, 'a short-lived love'. The transience of worldly phenomena is an important concept in Buddhism. Seeking permanence in the constantly changing is a source of anguish and pain for mankind.

Haikai: a form of linked verse where the opening poem of 5-7-5 syllables *hokku* stood separate from the rest.

Haiku: derived from *haikai no ku*. A seventeen syllable poem arranged in lines of 5-7-5 syllables. The name *haiku* gained currency in the Meiji Period (1868-1912).

Hanka: 'verse that repeats' derived from Chinese classical poetry in which the term referred to a similar auxiliary verse. The *hanka* or so-called *envoy* poems summarize, supplement or elaborate upon a long main poem – usually a *chōka*. Beautiful examples are to be found in *The Manyōshū*.

Hon'i: 'essential quality, a standard'. In poetry a recurring characteristic, for example, spring rain is linked with gentleness; in Homer's *Odyssey* the sea is always 'wine-dark'.

Kokoro: 'heart, feeling, spirit'. It includes mood, being touched by some emotional ambience, particularly in poetry.

Kotoba: language, speech, diction, and many aspects of the elements of speech and poetry. The expressive elements in a poem are contained in the concept *kotoba*.

Ku: 'a line, a verse, a poem, a stanza'.

Kū: 'an emptiness, a space'. The Buddhist conception of void in which no thing is. Importance is given in the meditation process to 'no-thought' or mental void.

Manyōshū: *The Manyōshū* is a collection of twenty books and contains over 4,000 poems. It is an anthology which reflects the life and times of Japan in the seventh and eighth centuries. The title is translated in various ways; examples are, 'Collection of Ten Thousand Leaves' and 'One Thousand Poems'.

Three kinds of verse feature in the compilation. Some ninety per cent are *tanka*. There are also examples of the so-called long poems or *chōka* which are accompanied by one or more *envoy* poems (auxiliary verses). There is a third form of poem, the *sedō ka* which later gradually fell into disuse.

The language is characterized by a frank directness in its references to the human condition and they usually carry a psychological emphasis rather than making a vague general statement. An excellent translation is available (see *Further Reading*).

Renku: a very long linked verse poem. Modern name for a *haikai* sequence by association with the term *renga*.

Renga: 'verse linking, a linked poem'. As a poetic form, dates from about the thirteenth century. Alternated patterns of 5-7-5 with 7-7 syllables.

Sabi: 'loneliness – tone of sadness and desolation'. A mood valued by mid-classical poets.

Sedōka: a verse-form comprising two sets of 5-7-5 syllables. About sixty examples occur in *The Manyōshū*. A rare form.

Shikan: 'organ of sight' hence insight and concentration. Discipline taught in Tendai Buddhism moving the mind away from analytical philosophy towards meditation and direct understanding. An approach adapted to poetic composition by some mid-classical poets.

Sonzai: 'existence, subsistence, being'. Linked with the Buddhist conception of the transience of all relative existence.

Tabi: 'travelling; a journey, a trip'. A subject of poetry from the early classical period; often an expression of sadness tinged with beauty.

Tanka: 'short poem' of thirty-one syllables in five lines 5-7-5-7-7. Also used as an *envoy* to *chōka* and as a partially discrete stanza within sequences. It is the major form of Japanese poetry.

Waka: a thirty-one syllable poem in five lines 5-7-5-7-7. Identical in form with the *tanka* but more formal and austere in content. Sometimes used as a synonym for *tanka*.

Yugen: 'mystery and depth' – an ideal of the mid-classical period. The name for a style associated with *sabi* and expressive of desolation and rich mysterious beauty, coupled with sadness.

Zazen: 'religious meditation; sit in meditation'. The master Kei-zan said, 'Zazen enables the practitioner to open up his mind, to see his own nature, to become conscious of the mysteriously pure and bright spirit or eternal light, within himself.'

Further Reading

The Arts Council of Great Britain, catalogue of exhibition *Sengai*, 1961.

Blyth, R.H. *A History of Haiku*, The Hokuseido Press, 1964.

Blyth, R.H. *Senryu*, The Hokuseido Press, 1949.

Keene, D. *Anthology of Japanese Literature*, Penguin Classics, 1955.

The Manyōshū, translated by N.G. Shinkokaim, Columbia University Press, 1965.

Miner, E. *An Introduction to Japanese Court Poetry*, Stanford University Press, 1968.

Miner, E. *Japanese Linked Poetry*, Princeton University Press, 1979.

Morris, I. *The Pillow Book of Sei Shōnagon*, Oxford University Press, 1967.

Stryk, L. and Ikemoto, T. *The Penguin Book of Zen Poetry*, Penguin Books, 1981.

Suzuki, D.T. *An Introduction to Zen Buddhism*, Grey Arrow edition, 1959.

Suzuki, S. *Zen Mind, Beginner's Mind*, Weatherhill, New York and Tokyo, 1981.

Yuasa, N. *The Narrow Road to the Deep North and other Travel Sketches*, Penguin Classics, 1966.